A Preacher's Guide

Colossians

Cover & Interior Design by Sean McCarthy, BasikMedia.net

ISBN 978-1-7327894-1-8

The New Life Church Preacher's Guide Series intends to strengthen and equip the work of preachers and teachers who labor faithfully in the ministry of God's Word.

Each guide is developed by members of New Life Church's teaching team and can be used as an aid to preaching, teaching, or small group study.

It is our hope that you and your team would be enriched by what you find here. Feel free to reach out to us with comments, suggestions, or questions (AArndt@newlifechurch.org).

Grace to you,

The New Life Church Teaching Team

Contents

Prepared By

Andrew Arndt

With contributions by: Dr. Glenn Packiam, Jason R. Jackson, Daniel Grothe, Amber Ayers, Brett Davis, and Andrew Arndt

Introduction

The City of Colossae

On the banks of the Lycus River in what is now modern Turkey sat the ancient city of Colossae. Of this city and the church to which the letter known as Colossians was addressed, the New Testament scholar J.B. Lightfoot remarked rather dryly: "Colossae was the least important church to which any epistle of St. Paul was addressed."[1] Lightfoot's comment perks our ears. That so great an epistle—towering in its vision of Christ, crucial in the history of Christian thought, revolutionary in its teaching—should emerge from the closed quarters of a prison cell, meandering thence to an utterly inconsequential city: surely this is one of the great hilarities of the New Testament. Or perhaps we should say: this sort of thing is the Incarnate God's signature.

The city's insignificance was not always so. Doug Moo notes that Colossae "was apparently the most important city in its vicinity in the 4th and 3rd centuries before Christ." Boasting a vibrant textile industry and located at the crossroads of two major ancient highways—one east/west connecting Ephesus and Sardis with the interior coast of Asia Minor, and another running north/south—Colossae was once regarded

---

1   As noted by Douglas J. Moo, *The Letters to the Colossians and to Philemon: PNTC* (Grand Rapids: Wm. B. Eerdmans Publishing Co. 2008), 26.

as "a great city" by the Greek historian Herodotus (*Hist.* 7.30.1).[2]

Part of its greatness no doubt lay in the tapestry of humanity it wove together. Moo comments:

> Its location on an important highway at a time of considerable mobility and the mixing of different ethnic groups that typified the Roman Empire meant that the population of Colossae was very diverse. A majority were undoubtedly Gentile, but we have good reason to think that there was also a substantial number of Jews. According to the Jewish historian Josephus, the Seleucid Ruler Antiochus III ("the Great") had settled two thousand Jewish families in the general area in 213 B.C. (*Antiquities* 12.3.4).[3]

In consequence, "Colossae was a place where many different religious and philosophical viewpoints thrived and probably mixed together"[4]—a situation not unlike our own. N.T. Wright characterizes Colossae as comprising

> ...its fair share of the variegated religious practices which characterized the Ancient Near East at this time. In this society the old gods of classical Greek culture still had their adherents, as did the 'mystery-religions' which promised entry to a secret, higher world for those who submitted to the proper initiation. With

---

2   Moo, 26.

3   Moo, 27.

4   Moo, 27.

the passage of time and the movement of people from one area to another, the lines between different cultures and religious ideas could get blurred, and the phenomenon known as 'syncretism'— the mixing of religious ideas and practices from a wide range of sources—became quite common.[5]

By the time of the New Testament, the greatness of Colossae was fading to distant memory. After the moving of the north-south highway from Colossae to nearby Laodicea (twelve miles west), the city's decline began in earnest. During the height of Paul's missionary activity in the province of Asia, both Laodicea and the northward city of Hierapolis (fifteen miles northwest) had surpassed it. When a major earthquake devastated the area in the early 60's A.D., the demise of Colossae was virtually sealed. Though eventually rebuilt, it would never attain its former glory. For centuries, this great cosmopolitan city of the ancient world has lain in ruins. No serious program of excavation has ever taken place.

Paul and the Colossian Church

In Paul's day, though Colossae's size and regional importance had waned, from all we can tell it nevertheless retained significant vestiges of the old culture—particularly in its ethnic, religious, and philosophical

---

5   N. T. Wright, *Colossians and Philemon: TNTC* (Downers Grove: InterVarsity Press, 1986), 24.

diversity. Perhaps surprisingly, we have no evidence that Paul ever visited the city, and we know for certain that he was not the founder of the church there, since he remarks that the Colossian believers are among all of those in the region of Asia Minor "who have not met me personally" (Col. 2:1). According to the letter, it was a man named Epaphras who had first brought the gospel to Colossae. "You learned it [the gospel]," Paul writes, "from Epaphras, our dear fellow servant, who is a faithful minister of Christ on our behalf, and who also told us of your love in the Spirit" (1:7-8).

But who was Epaphras? The little we can gather from the New Testament suggests that he was in all probability a convert of Paul's during the days of his nearly three-year ministry in Ephesus, as recorded in Acts 19. Luke notes the effectiveness of this season of Paul's ministry, saying that during this time "all the Jews and Greeks who lived in the province of Asia heard the word of the Lord" (Acts 19:10). Even if one were to grant a touch of hyperbole in Luke's writing, it is not difficult to imagine a scenario in which Epaphras, a native of Colossae (Col. 4:12), visiting the city of Ephesus, heard the gospel for the first time from the lips of the Apostle Paul and became both a follower of Jesus and a disciple of Paul's. He thereupon took the gospel back to Colossae, where a number of his friends, family, and neighbors became fellow believers. And so the church of the Colossians was born.

This scenario goes a long way to explain both the tender—almost familial—intimacy of the letter, as well as the authority the Apostle Paul demonstrates towards the Colossians, a group of people he had never met. This community in all likelihood felt like something of a granddaughter community to him—founded by one of his own converts, disciples, and dear friends, Epaphras. He carries them close to his heart: "For this reason, since the day we heard about you, we have not stopped praying for you" (1:9). He is willing to sacrifice for them: "Now I rejoice in what I am suffering for you, and I fill up in my flesh what is still lacking in regard to Christ's afflictions, for the sake of his body, which is the church" (1:24). And he is unafraid to challenge them: "Since you died with Christ to the elemental spiritual forces of the world, why, as though you still belonged to the world, do you submit to its rules?" (2:20). The Colossian believers were precious to Paul, who ached to see them "fully mature in Christ" (1:28).

The Threat of False Teaching

Accordingly, when the health of this beloved community came under threat, the pen of Paul went into motion. It seems that Epaphras, now feeling a bit over his head in dealing with erroneous teaching that had arisen in (or around) the young church, departed Colossae to visit Paul in prison, seeking his counsel. Judging by Paul's language in Philemon 23, Epaphras' visit became an inadvertent "extended stay"—Paul refers to him as a "fellow prisoner in Christ." Detained with Paul (scholars think that either nearby Ephesus or—much farther away—Rome is the likeliest location of their imprisonment), Epaphras would have had ample time to describe the precise nature of the Colossians' circumstances to his father in the faith, who then composed our epistle to both encourage and admonish the believers there, sending it by the hands of his much-beloved and trusted ministry partners, Tychicus and Onesimus (4:7-9). Paul's purpose in writing his letter is to draw attention to the growing threat, calling the faithful to remain "established and firm," unmoved "from the hope held out in the gospel" (1:23).

But just what was that threat?

The evidence of the letter, especially 2:8-23, suggests that it was some form of false teaching characterized *at least* by the following elements:[6]

1. It was a "hollow and deceptive philosophy" (v. 8), which *may* imply that the belief system and attendant practices were at least somewhat coherent (though that is disputed).

2. It depended on "human tradition" (v. 8; cf. v. 22), perhaps implying (based on similar language in Mark 7) that the false teaching was primarily Jewish in nature.

3. It depended on "elemental spiritual forces of this world" (v. 8), an ambiguous phrase that could mean any number of things depending on the context.

4. Crucially, as we will see, it did not "depend on Christ" (v. 8).

5. It included the observance of (apparently) Jewish food restrictions and also Jewish holy days (v. 16).

---

6   These eleven points are drawn from Moo, 50-51.

6. It advocated ascetic disciplines (v. 18; cf. v. 23). "False humility" is almost universally understood to be a reference to ascetic practices, perhaps as a form of preparation for mystical experiences (more on that to follow).

7. It focused some degree of its attention on angels (v. 18). Whether "the worship of angels" is human veneration of angels or the worship angels offer God is unclear.

8. It laid heavy emphasis on the supposed visions seen by the false teachers (v. 18).

9. The false teachers themselves were prideful people (v. 18).

10. The false teachers have also, in light of the foregoing, "lost connection with the head [of the body; that is, Christ]" (v. 19), imperiling themselves and others.

11. It propagated certain rules and restrictions as critical to the path of spiritual growth (vv. 20-23).

Given this wide range of characteristics, which make perfect sense in light of the profile of ethnic, religious, and philosophical diversity sketched above, it is easy to understand why no scholarly consensus exists as to what exactly the "Colossian heresy" was.

In general, four hypotheses have usually been advocated:[7]

1. **The false teaching is a primarily pagan philosophy** that encouraged cosmic speculation and ascetic practices in the pursuit of enlightenment or wisdom. This is a minority position largely because it fails to account for the obviously strong Jewish elements of the false teaching.

2. **The false teaching is pure Jewish legalism**, plain and simple. Under the influence of local synagogues, the (primarily Gentile) Colossian believers were feeling the pressure to "complete" the process begun in their conversion to Christ by becoming adherents of Judaism.[8] The strength of this position is that it takes into full account the Jewish elements of the text and also explains some of the similarities of Paul's critique in Colossians with critiques he launches elsewhere, such as Galatians 3-4, Romans 7:1-6, Philippians 3:2ff., and 2 Corinthians 3-5. Its weakness is the difficulty it has in explaining elements of the text that move obviously beyond the framework of Judaism.

3. **The false teaching is some form of Jewish mysticism**. A view that has seen a recent surge in popularity, the "Jewish mysticism" position does a nice job accounting for the close connection

---

7   David W. Pao, *Colossians and Philemon: Exegetical Commentary on the New Testament* (Grand Rapids: Zondervan, 2012), 27-31.

8   Wright in particular does a nice job advancing this thesis in his introduction to *Colossians and Philemon*.

between ascetic practices and spiritual experiences (such as the so-called "worship of angels"). It also would seem to form a background for some of what we see in the "Christ-hymn" of 1:15-20. Its weaknesses include an inability to account for the evil dimension of the heavenly powers we see in 2:15 and the complete lack of evidence we have in ancient literature for understanding "the worship of angels" as "the worship angels offer to God."

4. **The false teaching is some form of syncretism**—a blending of various philosophical and religious/cultic elements into a "new spiritual enthusiasm."[9] David Pao argues: "The evidence...appears to favor a syncretism with Jewish elements providing the controlling framework."[10] The strength of this view is that it accounts for all of the elements of the false teaching (listed above). The weakness is that not only do we *not* have any evidence in antiquity for the specific kind of syncretistic "philosophy" supposedly propounded by these false teachers, but the whole label ("syncretism") suffers from being too easy. *Of course* we're dealing with some form of syncretism—was there ever a religion or philosophy that existed in a "pure" form, free of contaminating elements? Hardly.

In the end, it is perhaps not so important that the preacher or teacher have a *label* for the false teaching as they do a basic understanding of its key elements. Moo provides an apt, but admittedly somewhat speculative, summary:

---

9   Joseph Dan quoted in Pao, 30.

10   Pao, 30.

The false teachers were probably people from within the Colossian Christian community who were bragging about their ability to find ultimate spiritual "fulfillment" via their own program of visions and asceticism. This program was drawn partly from Judaism, particularly in its focus on rules about eating and observing certain days. They were preoccupied with spiritual beings, probably because they viewed them as powerful figures capable of having significant influence on their lives. ...The false teachers were appealing to spiritual beings, visions, and rules to find security in this very uncertain universe.[11]

The main problem with this, according to Moo, was—and here we come to the point at issue:

In doing so, they were questioning the sufficiency of Christ. They may have done so directly, but it is more likely that their questions about Christ were implicit in their approach and that it is Paul who draws out the implications of this "philosophy" for Christology. The false teachers were so preoccupied with their own program for spiritual fullness that they were separating themselves from the only true source of spiritual power: the Lord Jesus Christ.[12]

He drives the point home:

Any teaching that questions the sufficiency of Christ—not only for

---

11   Moo, 59-60.
12   Moo, 60.

"initial" salvation but also for spiritual growth and ultimate salvation from judgment—*falls under the massive Christological critique of Colossians.*[13]

The parallels with our own day are impossible to miss. For we too—and perhaps more so than in the 1st century—live in a highly "syncretistic" culture in which people—some having grown weary of the Church's proclamation of the all-sufficiency of Christ, some unaware of it altogether—seek personal and spiritual fulfillment through a wide and blended variety of religious experiences, spiritualities, and philosophies, and we are easily enamored with the "spiritual guru" who has gone ahead of them on the path to fulfillment and can show them the way. The popularity of Eastern spiritualities, as well as figures like Deepak Chopra, the Dalai Lama, and many others, are ample evidence of this fact.

But it goes beyond that; it goes *deeper* than that. It is the *mood* of our age. We are a "Maslow's Hierarchy of Needs" culture ever vulnerable to the so-called "expert" who can help us climb the ladder of self-actualization, however we define it. We may not "delight in the worship of angels" in exactly the same way as the ancients did, but we certainly believe that there is a height of human experience available to us if we walk the right path, employ the right strategies, and organize our lives *just so.* Our lust for entry into the "mysteries" takes the form of fantasies of burgeoning bank accounts, tanned bodies, swanky dinner parties, and expensive vacations to the French Riviera—punctuated here and there

---

13   Moo, 60. Emphasis added.

with quiet moments of centering meditation to help us cultivate positive brain wave patterns. A materialist nirvana.

Our culture, as often as not, is nothing more than a half-hearted pastiche of the paganism of the ancient world, which was in its summer at the time of Paul's letter to the Colossians and is certainly experiencing something of a springtime today. And Paul's words therefore apply as pointedly to us as they did to the believers living in Colossae, facing pressures so similar to ours—pressures to seek solutions for life's vexing concerns outside of that which the Only God has provided in his Only Son, Jesus Christ our Lord. Paying careful attention both to the great themes and to the intricate detail of this magnificent book can help liberate our congregations afresh to know and grow up into the only "fullness" that God has ever or will ever provide—the Crucified and Resurrected One, Lord of all.

Themes

Accordingly, here are a few of the main themes to bear in mind as you read, interpret, and prepare to preach or teach Colossians.

The "Cosmic" Christ

Much has been made of the term "Cosmic Christ" in recent years, often by those seeking to propound one or another universalistic theology—the belief that all will finally be saved in the end. This is at least mildly ironic since the very point Paul is making with his "cosmic" Christological vision is arguably the exact opposite: *because* Christ is who he is, *therefore* those who seek fullness outside of him banish themselves to wrath (3:6).

Scholars describe Paul's Christological vision in Colossians as "cosmic" for good reason: it is simply the best summation of his thought in this densely packed epistle. Consider the great "Christ-hymn" of 1:15-20:

> The Son is the image of the invisible God,
>> the firstborn over all creation.
> For in him all things were created:
>> things in heaven and on earth,
>> visible and invisible,
>>> whether thrones or powers or rulers or authorities;
>> all things have been created through him and for him.
> He is before all things, and in him all things hold together.
> And he is the head of the body, the church;
> He is the beginning and the firstborn from among the dead,
>> so that in everything he might have the supremacy.
> For God was pleased to have all his fullness dwell in him,
>> and through him to reconcile to himself all things,
>>> whether things on earth or things in heaven,
>> by making peace through his blood, shed on the cross.

This is a vision of Christ as exalted as you will find in the New Testament. Paul here claims that the One who wrapped himself in human flesh, who was formed in Mary's womb, who suffered hunger and thirst, pain and weariness, who tasted doubt and struggle in Gethsemane, whose innocent blood was spilled at Golgotha is, in fact, none other than the Father's exact "image," the One through whom and for whom all things were made and in whom all things "hold together." He is, in other words, Lord of Creation and all things therein—whether visible or invisible. Indeed, Paul asserts, having died our death and raised again to new life—set beyond the reach of death forever—he stands exalted as Lord of the *New* Creation and Head of the Church, for the fullness of God dwells in him and through him all things are reconciled. This man and no other, Jesus, holds it all together. Now and forever.

It is for this reason that Paul can say with such great confidence that the Colossian believers have nothing to fear—either visible or invisible—and nothing to seek outside of this Christ, in whom "all the fullness of the Deity lives in bodily form," for "in Christ you have been brought to fullness" (2:9-10). Every power in heaven and on earth is subject to Christ who is Lord over all, which means that there is nothing—no wisdom, no knowledge, no spiritual experience, no enlightenment, no moral strength, no cleanness of conscience—to be had outside of Christ. Our deepest desire for contact with the "really real," with Reality itself, finds its fulfillment in Christ: "These [ascetic practices and Jewish rituals]," Paul asserts, "are a shadow of the things that were to come; the reality, however, is found in Christ" (2:17). To touch him is to touch the very depth of reality—God of very God. Everything else is, at best, a shadow cast by the Substance that is Christ the Lord.

The Gospel

Accordingly, the gospel is a prominent theme in Colossians. The word for "gospel" is the Greek word *euangellion*—literally a "good message" in the sense that it is *news* about something that had happened which is a cause for great joy. In the ancient world the word was often used to announce a military victory or the accession of a new leader to the throne—both, in their way, a cause for rejoicing insofar as the nation was thereby secured anew.

When the New Testament writers use the term to describe what God has accomplished for us in Jesus, they use it in almost exactly this sense. The gospel is the "good message" about the entry of God in the person of Christ onto our battle-scarred turf, conquering sin and death, along with every other power that stands against humanity, by his own death, securing us anew in resurrection life. In the "true word of the gospel" (1:5) human beings have access into the new realities brought into being by the death and resurrection of Jesus.

The message of the gospel, therefore, has what we might call a "sacramental" quality. In these human words that attest to the Living Word, the Living Word himself becomes present and powerful. The life of God is released into the world through the gospel of Jesus Christ. And so it is that Paul lays heavy emphasis on the spiritual importance and practical centrality of the gospel in Colossians:

> ...the faith and love that spring from the hope stored up for you
> in heaven and about which you have already heard in the true

message of the *gospel* (1:5)

...the *gospel* is bearing fruit and growing throughout the whole world—just as it has been doing among you (1:6)

...to present you holy in his sight, without blemish and free from accusation—if you continue in your faith, established and firm, and do not move from the hope held out in the *gospel*. This is the *gospel* that you heard and that has been proclaimed to every creature under heaven (1:22-23)

And so forth. And even where the word *euangellion* is not explicitly mentioned, it is implied throughout:

...to present to you the *word of God* in its fullness...Christ in you, the hope of glory (1:25, 27)

[Christ] is the one we *proclaim*...so that we may present everyone fully mature in Christ (1:28)

...rooted and built up in [Christ], strengthened in the faith *as you were taught* (2:7)

Let the *message of Christ* dwell among you richly as you teach and admonish one another with all wisdom through psalms, hymns, and songs from the Spirit, singing to God with gratitude in your hearts (3:16)

Paul's working assumption is that the *message about what God has done in Jesus* conveys to the hearers *the reality of what God has done in Jesus*. Therefore, the community of faith is called to hold fast to the message, to meditate on the message, to mine the richness of the message, to guard the message from the error of additions that pollute it—in all, to let the true word of the gospel become its very aura. This is the very best, indeed, the only hope the church has to advance in spiritual maturity.

The Church

No one who reads Colossians carefully can fail to notice the close association Paul makes between Christ and his Church. The great St. Augustine once described God as "the Life of the life of my soul"[14] and this would certainly be one very good way to begin to think about the association between Christ and the Church in Colossians. "*Christ in you, the hope of glory*" is how Paul summarizes the message that he and his companions have been proclaiming to all who will hear (1:27) with the goal of presenting everyone "fully mature in Christ" (1:28). And he does so laboring "with all the energy Christ so powerfully works in me" (1:29).

Christ is not just *Lord over* but is *present within* his Church as its animating presence, its ongoing source of power and life. And so he is called the "head of the body, which is the church" (cf. 1:18; 1:24).

---

14   St. Augustine, *Confessions*. Book X, Chapter 6.

Moo notes, "How Paul arrived at the notion of the church as Christ's body is debated. But almost surely involved was the idea of Christ as a 'corporate person,' one who, like Adam in the Old Creation, represents the totality of God's New Creation."[15] Just as once we were "in Adam"—in the realm of sin, slavery, and death; so now we are "in Christ"—in the realm of righteousness, freedom, and life.

To be "in Christ" is to be in the New Creation. And this is precisely what Paul says in 2 Corinthians 5:17—"Therefore, if anyone is in Christ, the new creation has come!" The Church therefore is that place in the midst of the Old Creation where the New Creation can be seen, touched, interacted with. "As there is a single 'creation' over which Christ rules, so there must be a single, all-inclusive 'new creation,' a 'church' (ekklesia) where—and only where—Christ can be known, worshipped, and proclaimed."[16] The Church, incorporated by faith into Christ, is the place in the Old Creation where the New shines through—dimly at times, but surely.

Which is why Paul is so emphatic that the Colossian believers remain in Christ: "So then, just as you received Christ Jesus as Lord, continue to live your lives in him, rooted and built up in him, strengthened in the faith as you were taught, and overflowing with thankfulness" (2:6-7). The lives of the Colossian believers are now "hidden with Christ in God" (3:3) and will be revealed as such at the eschaton: "When Christ, who is your life (recall the Augustine quote), appears, then you also will appear

---

15   Moo, 67.

16   Moo, 66.

with him in glory" (3:4).

An enormous part of this is the congregation's manner of behavior, and Paul wastes no words exhorting them accordingly. They must put to death behaviors that belong to the Old Creation (3:5-10) and act as those who have stepped into a new way of being human, made possible in Christ (cf. the "new self" in 3:10-11), clothing themselves with virtues and deeds that belong to the kingdom of the beloved Son (3:12-17). This includes how they behave in their homes: wives and husbands, children and parents, masters and slaves are all summoned to calibrate their relationships to the Lordship of Christ (3:18-4:1).

Further, the "in Christ-ness" of the community will be shown in their ongoing participation in the mission of evangelism. They are to keep watch in prayer (4:2), remembering Paul and his companions before the Lord and pleading for grace over their missionary efforts (4:3-4), conducting themselves in their behavior towards outsiders in ways that are "salty" (4:6).

If this seems a scandal—that God would invest so much in fallible human beings—then perhaps we preachers and teachers should simply lean into it. The great 20th century missiologist Lesslie Newbigin once called the church the "hermeneutic of the gospel"[17]—a genuinely Pauline idea. When the community of faith lives its life in Christ, when its members honor and serve one another, when they speak words

---

17   Lesslie Newbigin, *The Gospel in a Pluralist Society* (Grand Rapids: Wm. B. Eerdmans Publishing Co., 1989), 227.

that heal and bless, when they live uprightly, when they welcome the stranger and take care of the orphan and widow, when they, in short, let the New Creation made possible in Christ shine forth, then—and only then—is their message credible.

May it be in our day.

1:1-14

Introduction And Prayer

(Jason Jackson)

Paul opens his letter to the Colossians in characteristic form. He establishes his authority as an apostle, credits his co-author, identifies his audience, and extends God's grace and peace to them. On this occasion (as noted in the Introduction) he writes to a church he neither founded nor visited. They know each other through Epaphras (vv. 7-8). Paul describes his readers as those "in Christ in Colossae." As Wright elucidated, "To be described as 'in Christ' and 'in Colossae' is to be located with precision in the purposes of God, as a member both of his true people and of that particular earthly community where one is called to service and witness."[1]

Then, as he often does, Paul recounts his prayers for the community. Paul's prayers are practically instructive, liturgically beneficial, and exegetically illuminating. They arise from his concerns for the church and foreshadow his arguments and instructions. As mentioned in the Introduction, Paul pens this letter to oppose teachings that question the supremacy of Christ and to encourage the Colossian believers to remain faithful. Correspondingly, he gives thanks for their gospel receptivity (vv.

---

1   Wright, 51-52.

3-8) and intercedes for their continued growth and patient endurance (vv. 9-14).

Paul praises their *faith* in Jesus, their *love* for the Church, and their *hope* in the kingdom (vv. 4-5). This isn't the first time he has connected these virtues (see 1 Cor. 13:13, 1 Thess. 1:3 and 5:8); here he describes them as the fruits of the gospel (v. 6). His depiction recalls Jesus' parable of the sower (Matt. 13:3-21, Mark 4:3-20, and Luke 8:4-15). In this story, the sower liberally sows seeds of the gospel, but only some of the seeds fall on good soil where the gospel sprouts, develops deep roots, grows tall shoots, and bears abundant fruit. Ultimately, fruitfulness is the distinguishing feature of the good soil. It is the ultimate goal of the gospel and measure of discipleship.

Paul ceaselessly prays the Colossians will be filled with the knowledge of God's will (v. 9) so that they may live worthy (Greek—*axios*) lives (v. 10). He uses the same word in Ephesians 4:1. "I encourage you to live as people *worthy* of the call you received from God" (CEB). Paul wants the Colossians to know what God is doing so that they can join God's work. This looks like bearing more fruit, growing in knowledge, being strengthened to endure, and giving thanks (vv. 10-11). As Wright explains, these verses "form a miniature picture of Christian life and growth. The argument is not circular (as might at first appear), but spiral. Paul prays that they may increase in knowledge of God's will, with the result that the Colossians will live as God wants them to and so increase in the knowledge of God! Understanding will fuel holiness;

holiness will deepen understanding."[2]

Preaching Pathways

1. **Love for the church.** As he does elsewhere, Paul associates faith, hope, and love. For him, these virtues live together. Here Paul particularly notes the Colossians' love for the Church (v. 4). We live in a time where faith in Christ and love for his people are frequently disassociated—where personal faith no longer lives in the community of faith but is frequently, intentionally, and even pridefully dislocated from the Church. The privatization of faith is foreign to Paul and the rest of the Scriptures.

2. **Gospel fruit.** The gospel is generative. It produces something in us that comes out of us. What it produces generates even more. Its fruit contains seeds that grow and bear more fruit. This is its ecology. As Jesus notes, we are soil in which the gospel grows. The state of our soil matters. Our continued openness and faithfulness to the gospel's work in us will either enable or inhibit its fruitfulness.

3. **Gratitude.** Paul concludes his prayer in verse 12 by asking for the Colossians to give thanks (Greek—*eucharisteo*). He mentions the importance of thanksgiving four other times in this letter (1:3, 2:7, 3:17, and 4:2). Gratitude is fueled by remembering what God has

---

2   Wright, 63.

accomplished in Christ and is continuing to accomplish through the Spirit. Subsequently, gratitude fuels faithfulness. The moment we stop giving thanks we start thinking we need something or someone else.

4. **The prayer and the poem.** Paul follows his prayer with a poem about the centrality and supremacy of Jesus (1:15-20). If the Colossians are going to bear fruit, if they are going to mature, if they are going to patiently resist false teaching, then they must know and remember Jesus. The prayer and the poem work together to reinforce Paul's central argument—stick with Jesus.

1:15-2:5

Christus: Lord Of The Old And The New

(Andrew Arndt)

Fourteen verses into this magnificent book and we come to one of the most beloved and exalted passages in all the New Testament: the "Christ-hymn" of Colossians 1:15-20. Paul is no stranger to showing off his poetic chops—especially when it serves his central theological agenda—and these verses are a fine example of that. Here we see Paul's lyrical theology in full flight.

The passage builds off of the previous verses, where Paul has both expressed his gratitude for the Colossian believers (vv. 3-8) and also given them a glimpse into his ongoing prayer for them (vv. 9-14). Verses 13 and 14 conclude with a description of what God the Father has done for his saints—rescuing them from the dominion of darkness and transferring them into the kingdom of his beloved Son, "in whom," Paul says, "we have redemption, the forgiveness of sins." God's saving work in the person of Christ has now taken center stage. The question Paul will ask, and answer, is: "Just who is this Christ, who is called 'Son'?"

Bearing that in mind, it is worth pointing out that whereas in the NIV verse 15 begins with *"He [the Son] is,"* the Greek is more explicit: *"Hos estin..."*—literally: *"Who is."* The marker alerts us to the fact that Paul is about to advance a more robust description of this figure, Christ, whom he has just recently introduced. There is a great deal to be learned in verses 15-20 (let the wise interpreters consult their commentaries). Here we will just point out that the poem breaks neatly into two sections, which correspond to Paul's theological agenda:

> Verses 15-17, which detail the Son's identity as the very "image" of God and the Lord of what we might call the "First Creation."

> Verses 18-20, which detail the Son's identity as the Head of the Church, the Firstborn from among the dead, the One in whom the fullness of God was pleased to dwell, and therefore the Lord of the New Creation.

Paul's point could hardly be clearer: Christ, who is the image of God and in whom the fullness of God dwells, is also the One through whom all things were made and by whose death and resurrection all things are reconciled. To step outside of Christ is not an advance from one spiritual dimension to a *higher* one. It is not, really, even a step from one spiritual dimension to *another* one. It is a step into sheer nothingness— into the First (or Old) Creation, which was judged in his body on the cross and is passing away into nonbeing.

Accordingly, Paul turns his attention back again to the Colossian believers, reminding them that by virtue of their faith they have tasted of this great reconciliation achieved in Christ. They have stepped into the New Creation, and therefore they must *continue in it*, for the message about Christ is the only genuine gospel that ever will or can be preached to a world so desperate for healing (vv. 21-23). The advance of this gospel, Paul tells the Colossians, has been his singular concern. It is what he suffers for and serves, aching to see the mystery proclaimed so that men and women everywhere might be presented mature in Christ (vv. 24-28). He doesn't labor in this emptily—it is Christ himself who contends for this exact goal in and through Paul (v. 29). And it is not just for the Colossians that Paul is concerned. He aches even "for all who have not met me personally" (2:1) that the body of Christ would rise up, united and whole, everywhere (vv. 2-3).

It is at just this point that Paul sounds the first note of concern: *"I tell you this so that no one may deceive you by fine-sounding arguments"* (2:4). What we have heard so far has a purpose: to delineate the truth so that falsehood, however beautifully dressed, may be more easily discerned. The rest of Chapter 2 will be devoted to contrasting this truth with the false teaching making its rounds in Colossae.

Preaching Pathways

1. **Christ: Lord of the Old and the New**. Colossians 1:15-20 is as clear and compelling a statement as one is likely to find in the New Testament on Christ's identity with the Father and Lordship over both Old and New Creations. Preach the depth and breadth of it with passion!

2. **The Church: wrapped up in the mystery.** Where in the midst of the

Old Creation is the New Creation to be found? The answer Paul consistently gives—not just in Colossians but throughout his writings—is: "In the Church." Paul sees the Church unavoidably wrapped up in the mystery of the Resurrected Christ's presence and Lordship. He is the "head" of the "body" that is the Church, indwelling and guiding her. This is a marvelous opportunity to present a very "high" view of the local church.

3. **Christ: the Goal and the Means of maturity.** Accordingly, the drum that Paul beats again and again in Colossians is that the community of faith need look nowhere else for maturity. He is both the Goal ("everyone fully mature in Christ") and the Means ("Christ in you, the hope of glory").

4. **Mission: "filling up" the afflictions of Christ.** For Paul, this is a way of talking about the sacrifices he makes to see to it that Christ gets all—everyone and everything—that belongs to him. What are we willing to sacrifice? And for whom?

2:6-15

Filled By The Fullness

(Brett Davis)

The solar system exists in orbit around Sol—our sun. Without that defining center, order would erode, chaos ensue, life disappear. In proper orbit, however, all things flourish. Having established for his listeners the center of the universe (1:15-20), Paul is now imploring them to remain stable in their orbit around Jesus (1:23ff.). That's the living pulse of Paul's thought here: remain *"rooted and built up"* (v. 7) in the incarnate, crucified, resurrected, and cosmic Son. Don't stray from the Son.

Some kind of false thinking and living has crept into the church at Colossae (see Introduction). There is no scholarly consensus on what, precisely, this philosophical or "religious" teaching was, and this ambiguity is likely a gift to the preacher and the church present. The "thorn" that Paul struggles with elsewhere (2 Cor. 12:7) would lose its universal power were it explicitly named ("Paul struggled with his eyesight, but I struggle with ____"). So, too, these philosophical and religious/cultic temptations would lose their comprehensive quality if they were fully and finally nameable. The struggles of Colossae (be they Gnostic, Neoplatonic, Jewish mysticism, mystery cults, etc.) serve as a mirror to recognize the innumerable ways the Church may drift from its orbit around the Triune God revealed by the Son. And drift inevitably results in slavery (v. 8).

The answer to their physical and psychological temptations (and ours) is not a better system of "sin management."[1] Rather, the solution lies in *recognizing* reality's center and *remaining* in intimate orbit with God-revealed-in-Jesus. Paul affirms their hunger for spiritual knowledge...and redirects it (vv. 8-9). Our hunger is not the problem; the problem comes when we feast on a mirage. So Paul points them to the banquet of Christ in verses 9-10: "For in Christ all the fullness [pleroma] of the Deity lives in bodily form, and in Christ you have been brought to fullness [*pepleromenoi*]." In many competing forms of thinking (Gnosticisms, etc.) the *pleroma* was the fullest spiritual perfection of all divine powers and possibilities; *pleroma* was the magnificent, mysterious goal many were pursuing. Paul insists that the Goal behind all possible goals has been revealed (surprisingly as humble, self-emptying love), and this Goal has already found us. The impossible finish line has come forward to find us, the cripples crawling backwards. The "powers" (v. 15, cf. v. 8)—both spiritual powers and their earthly manifestations—have been rendered powerless by the passion of the *pleroma* (v. 14). The Living Feast has already found us and invites us to eat and be filled with fullness. Those satiated with Reality will not chase mirages.

God's saving work, of course, involves present, "enfleshed" realities and not merely future hope. The plural verbs throughout are worth noting.

---

1   See Chapter 2 of Dallas Willard's *The Divine Conspiracy* (New York: Harper, 1998) for a life-changing shift on how we make the gospel about "sin management" instead of about new, eternal, kingdom life.

The gravity of Jesus pulls us out of *an isolated deadness* and into an orbit of *aliveness in relationship* (v. 13). An orbit orders us so we can be "us." Our being given a "circumcision" (v. 11) signals our inclusion in the community of God's people—it involves our entire self-centered self being "put off." Like Eustace the Dragon being torn apart by Aslan in C. S. Lewis' *The Voyage of the Dawn Treader*, God slays us (cf. v. 20, 3:3) so that we can be made alive (v. 13) and, together, practice becoming our true selves (cf. 3:5, 3:10). We practice the salvation-life in community... not in isolation. Our baptism (v. 12) is an immersion into the endless, delighting life of Father, Son, and Spirit *through* the living body of the Son, the Church (cf. v. 19, 1:18).

Paul calls us to *recognize* and *remain* in the cosmic, divine fullness that has now, already, by grace filled *you*. Or, to put a colloquial spin on Paul's language: *filled y'all* (the Church). Believe him. And don't stop. Stay in orbit and all things flourish.

Preaching Pathways

1. **The "pleroma" as self-emptying love.** There's a treasure trove to explore in the ancient notion of "pleroma" and the way that Paul insists that it has been unmasked and actually arrived in the life of Jesus. And it's full of tension and paradox, because "the Divine

fullness" is revealed as a Divine emptying or "kenosis."[2] Fullness of life is found in kenotic love. This love has already found us, and we're called to embody it—that's where we experience fullness of life.

2. **From modern syncretism to orbiting Jesus.** There's an opportunity here for the preacher to springboard from the ancient cultural atmosphere to current cultural atmosphere, from Neoplatonism to nationalism, from Gnosticism to consumerism, from mystery cults to relativism. And there's also an opportunity to let a robust view of Jesus help us discern what is true (and false) in our cultural atmospheres.

3. **Grace as central to salvation.** Verses 10-14 contain implicitly what Ephesians 2:8-9 declare explicitly: salvation is entirely a work of grace preceding anything we do. The gospel is an unconditional promise that I am invited to believe as true *for me*. Preach grace and preach it hard. God's grace changes lives and raises the dead.

4. **Relationship as central to salvation.** The plural verbs for salvation are begging us to recognize that God's salvation comes to the world in a group of people—the Church. We're grated into a group, into a body. Relationships are not an optional add-on; they're the very

---

2 Theologians use the word *kenosis* as a shorthand to talk about the "self-emptying" of Jesus that Paul refers to in Philippians 2:5-11; specifically verse 6, where Paul says that Christ "made himself nothing" (NIV), which is a translation of the Greek *ekenosen*.

substance of God's salvation. We are saved for relationship (with God and others) and through relationship (with God and others).

2:16-23

Shadows And Substance

(Brett Davis)

Plato tells a famous story in which people are imprisoned in a cave and have never seen the real world or anything in it.[1] These prisoners can only see the cave wall in front of them. Quite often, however, they see shadows of the real world—shadows of trees or men or puppets. These prisoners, however, cannot see the substance casting the shadows. And because they have never left the cave, the shadows are the deepest, truest reality they can imagine. The shadows are everything, and the shadows are nothing.

Paul borrows this common language and conceptual framework[2] when he refers to various religious practices as mere "shadows" (*skia*) of a solid "body" (*soma*). Jesus, however, has shown us "the thing itself": the "body," not just the "shadows" (v. 17). That is Paul's answer to those obsessing, judging, and dividing over religious trivialities (v. 16). Humankind could previously only make distorted, two-dimensional guesses about ultimate reality. Now, however, guesswork is gone. The

---

1   The famous allegory of the cave can be found in Plato's "Republic."

2   Andrew Lincoln, *Colossians, Vol. 11: TNIB* (Nashville: Abington Press, 2000), 631. "Such a comparison, deriving from Platonic thought, was common in Hellenistic writings, including Hellenistic Jewish texts."

crucified-yet-alive Messiah doesn't just point us toward ultimate reality; he actually *is* ultimate reality (cf. Col. 1:15-20; Heb. 1:1-3). The shadow of our Lover is a good thing; the embrace of our Lover is incomparably better. And we have been blissfully made one flesh with the "body" of our Lover (v. 19, cf. 1:18).

Controversially, Paul singles out the ancient devotional practices of the people of God. Festivals, new moons, and Sabbath (v. 16) "are typical of the way Jews, not least out in the Gentile world, tried to order their life of worship."[3] Even the Sabbath—and indeed the Jewish scriptures themselves (cf. Heb. 10:1)—were only shadows of ultimate reality. But something better has come close to the people of God—God himself. On a first date a couple might use "icebreaker questions" to foster conversation, and they'll certainly exchange phone numbers at some point to help foster connection. But icebreaker questions and phone numbers—good and necessary as their role may be—find no place in the marriage bed. A different kind of knowing outshines them. In similar fashion, the best directional, devotional practices fade when God actually, intimately arrives. And arrive God has—in Christ. When we recognize ourselves as both dying with Jesus (v. 20) and raised to life with Jesus (3:1), we're arriving to the marriage bed. The practices (vv. 17-18, 21-23) that may have once been appropriate become foolish when we confuse them with our Beloved. The relationship is the reality; the "rules" are devotional shadows and directional signs.

---

3   N.T. Wright, *Paul for Everyone: The Prison Letters* (Louisville: Westminster John Knox Press, 2015), 171.

The centuries have defused neither the danger nor the delight of Paul's explosive claim. Many could take Paul's radical rejection of religious regulation as invitation to indulge ourselves in selfishness and sin (cf. Rom. 6:1). Proclaiming the unconditional promise of the gospel always carries the danger of being misunderstood. (We know we are getting close to unspeakable goodness of the gospel when people start asking these questions.) But we are called—in the same breath—to a life that rejects both empty religious regulations, as well as the emptiness of "sensual indulgence" (v. 23). Ironically, selfishness drives humankind to a form of religion (v. 23: ethelothréskia, literally "desire-religion" or "will-worship") as well as the vices soon outlined in 3:5-9a. Both belong to a system that does not last (v. 22, cf. "the earth" in 3:5). The invitation of the gospel promise is to substance—to real, true, lasting life. And that life—this "pleroma" (cf. 1:19, 2:9)—always looks like self-emptying love for the good of others. In fact, it is identical with it. The Substance is the Christ who emptied himself, and "substantive" living therefore always looks like him.

Preaching Pathways

1. **The realest real.** Hone in on the language of "shadows." Shadows are pointers, clues about something more true, solid, and real than the shadow itself. Our religious impulses certainly fit into this category. But there's also an opportunity to uncover *all* our longings and desires as "shadows" of the real touching our lives. We long for Beauty, Justice, Truth, Goodness—we long for God—in all we do.

Even our sins are just our pursuit of the good in deficient, defective ways. Name the shadows in order to point to the Substance.

2. **The mystical encounter.** The "Cosmic Christ" introduced in 1:15-20 looms large over all of Chapter 2. There's space here to invite the faithful into deep communion with the Spirit of Christ. It's the difference between reading about a romance and encountering the Other in intimate union. Let verses 17 and 19 guide you here.

3. **Kill the sacred cows.** If you want to make changes in the church for the sake of the gospel, here's your text. Paul blows that conversation wide open and challenges us not to fight over trivial religious silliness. God raised Jesus from the dead, for crying out loud—let's kill the cows and get about the business of the kingdom.

4. **Self-indulgent religion.** That word ethelothréskia (v. 23, literally "desire-religion" or "will-worship") only shows up here and nowhere else in the New Testament. What are the ways in which our spirituality might be masking selfishness? Are we being "puffed up" by our practices? Use this moment to reframe spiritual disciplines as the places where we can cultivate the self-emptying (kenosis) made possible by the Spirit of the crucified Messiah.

3:1-11

New Life With Christ

(Amber Ayers)

The theme of *new life*, which figures prominently in this text, is a repeated refrain throughout Scripture. No wonder so many churches adopt variations of that refrain in their official name. It signifies leaving old ways behind and re-orienting our whole lives toward Christ.

Paul dramatically splits the old life from the new life with *death and resurrection* imagery. Dying with Christ (2:20; 3:3) symbolizes the drastic separation from the old life and forms the foundation for Paul's warnings against the rules of a "hollow and deceptive philosophy" (2:8) threatening the Colossians believers. Rising with Christ (3:1) emphasizes the new status of those who place their faith in Christ and refers to the power source for living the new way of life.[1]

This new life begins when we set our hearts on things above, not on earthly things (v. 1). Like Jesus' exhortation to seek first his kingdom (Matt. 6:33), the action of setting our hearts on heavenly things is parallel to seeking the kingdom of God. There is a hiddenness (v. 3) and

---

1   David E. Garland, *The NIV Application Commentary: Colossians and Philemon* (Grand Rapids: Zondervan, 1998), 201.

mystery about the kingdom of God that is *already* here, but *not yet* in its fullness. As participants in the *here-and-now-but-also-coming* kingdom, our new lives will be a secret truth, hidden from the view of others.

In verse 5, Paul shifts gears, transitioning into the heart of the letter's ethical appeal. He minces no words. The word "therefore" (v. 5) indicates that the following commands are dependent on the previous statement. New life in Christ, which will be fully experienced on the last day (v. 4), is to be manifested in the present time in the ways that Christians conduct themselves. The verbs "put to death" (v. 5) and "rid yourselves" (v. 8) tee up two lists of vices, one relating to sexual sin, the other to sins of anger. Again, a stark contrast is drawn between the list of vices (vv. 5-10) and the list of virtues (vv. 12-14). Like taking off an old, stained, grimy shirt and throwing it in the trash, the Colossians are exhorted to cast off the old self with its practices and put on the new, clean wardrobe.

Central to Paul's exhortations are commands related to speech. Paul knew that the right words could bring a neighbor into the family of God or send them running in the opposite direction. In 1st century Colossae no less than in our day, what we say and how we say it has a significant impact on our relationships. James reminds us that the tongue is one of the toughest members of our bodies to master, and it reveals what is going on inside of us (James 3:1-12).

In setting forth these ethical ideals, Paul is not inviting us to simply ponder them, but rather to *live* them. And Paul grounds his exhortation in Christology, the Person of Christ. We are being transformed into

Christ's image (v. 10) as we leave behind the old life and take up the new life.[2]

Rounding out this section, Paul breaks down the divisions of race, ancestral religion, class and caste. Drawing these dividing lines only leads to the mutual suspicion and distrust which warp into the vices previously listed (v. 8).[3] With breathtaking challenge, Paul points out that these distinctions deny the creation of humankind in the image of God. Instead, Christ is all, and in all. (v. 11).

Preaching Pathways

1. **Christ is our life.** Remember the T-shirt that said, "Swimming Is Life," worn by the chlorine-smelling, bleach-haired teenager who spent many hours a day in the pool? For a Christ-follower to say, "Christ is my life," is to say that all meaning is found in and through Christ. He is the most important thing in life; he *is* life. This is the peak of devotion.[4]

2. **We become what we think and feel.** We are inadvertently molded by the passions of our hearts.[5] Our attention, energy and time

---

2   Garland, 204.

3   Wright, 139.

4   William Barclay, *The New Daily Study Bible: The Letters to the Philippians, Colossians and Thessalonians* (Louisville: Westminster John Knox Press, 2003), 173.

5   Lloyd John Ogilvie, *You Are Loved and Forgiven* (Ventura: Regal Books, 1977), 136.

can become focused on our agenda and our priorities rather than the things of God. But as our minds are renewed (Rom. 12:2) and our hearts are made new (Psa. 51:10), our actions and behavior patterns will take a different shape. This transformation is only accomplished through the work of the Holy Spirit and by the grace of God.[6]

3. **Laying aside the old life and taking up the new life is a renewal process, best worked out in community.** This renewal process is energized by leaning into community. Arrogant *independence* produces the conduct found in verses 5-11, fed by the rampant individualism and isolationism in our culture. But loving *interdependence* produces the behavior found in verses 12-17, reinforced and upheld in healthy community.

4. **Our speech should bring life.** Some guiding questions can help steer our speech towards that which brings life.[7] We can ask: Is it pure? Is it true? Is it necessary? Is it kind? Is it helpful?

---

6   One powerful practice that you might consider recommending to your congregation is the Prayer of Examen, which is an ancient way of encountering God in everyday life. At the end of the day, ponder these things: "What consumed my thoughts today? Where was my focus and attention?" Look over the major experiences of the day and your responses to them. What interior moods, feelings, urges, reactions, emotions and/or thought patterns are associated with the experiences? See www.ignatianspirituality.com/ignatian-prayer/the-examen for more instructions and guiding questions.

7   Gary Demarest, *Colossians: The Mystery of Christ in Us* (Waco: Word, Incorporated, 1979), 154.

3:12-4:1

Practicing This New Life

(Glenn Packiam)

We've all had beginnings that feel like the start of a new life: the first day at a new school, the start of a new job, a wedding day, a graduation, or even the birth of a child. You get the sense that Paul is summoning every association we have to significant life changes and turning the volume all the way up. "You're brand new!" he seems to exclaim. But this isn't just a newness that results from new life circumstances. This newness is like resurrection: it is not an achievement; it is a gift. The risen Christ has raised us up to new life (3:1). Yet far from being the end of the story with nothing left for us to do, it is a beginning of a new way of living. Paul wants us to *participate* in this newness by *practicing* a new kind of life. *Grace is found not only in the gift of new life but in the invitation to live in a new way.*

In the previous verses, Paul tells us what to "put to death" and "put away" (vv. 5, 8). Now, he wants us to know what to "put on" (v. 12). "Putting on" is usually used to describe a fake or pretentious person, but the verb here has a plain meaning in other usage: it describes putting on clothing. (That's why some translations say, "Clothe yourselves...") Like a uniform for a soldier, like scrubs for a surgeon, like a wedding dress for the bride and a tux for the groom, there are new clothes to match this new life. To contrast the five vices Paul has told us to take off, he now gives five virtues to "put on." Compassion. Kindness. Humility. Gentleness. Patience.

As with all of Paul's lists, this is not meant to be exhaustive or definitive; it's a sketch to get us started. What is most remarkable about these virtues is that, unlike the Greek virtues, these are not abstract moral goods to strive toward; these are attributes of God on particular display in Christ Jesus. The Greeks believed in training yourself toward virtue, practicing habits that formed you for a flourishing life. The Romans switched the goal slightly, making the goal of virtue-formation the preparation to be a good citizen, or even to rule. But what Paul is up to is completely different. We are to put on these things because *this is what Christ is like! The new life we have received is Christ's life; the new way we are to live is also Christ's life.*

If the passage ended here, we may be left wondering what this really looks like in practice. Yes, Jesus lived this way and we can look to his life, but what might compassion, kindness, humility, gentleness, and patience look like in our lives, in our relationships with others? Paul answers this through a series of exhortations about three pairs of relationships usually seen in a single household. "Household codes," as these passages are sometimes called, go back at least to Aristotle, who uses these same three pairs. Paul's version of household codes acknowledges the norms of his day and doesn't see them as inherently contradictory to the Christians' call to live as if each person in Christ is their equal (see v. 11). While we should be cautious about baptizing these structures as God's intended design—in fact, they were the household structures of the unbelieving world—we must also be careful not to say that Christian practice is incompatible with such structures. The point is that *regardless of where you find yourself, in the place of power or not, there is a way for you to practice compassion, kindness, humility, gentleness, and patience.*

It is also worth noting that in all three pairs, it is likely that the head of the household was in the place of power: he is the husband, the father, and the master. This is where Paul's household codes are most distinguished from their secular or pagan counterparts: He is unflinching in his admonishment for the head of the household to be loving, kind, gentle, and just. *Near the center of our new life in Christ, we see that power has been repurposed.* Strength is for service.

For all the need to practice this new life through putting off certain ways and putting on new ones, we must be careful not to miss what lies at the heart of this passage: the exhortation to allow the Word of Christ to dwell in us (v. 16). The only way that such a new life is possible is because of the Word of Christ. *When Christ speaks, his words do not simply issue a command; they create the power to obey the command.* And so, we are to *"let* the Word of Christ dwell in us richly." Even as we practice putting on compassion and kindness and humility and gentleness and patience within the various relationships and power structures, it is the Word of Christ that makes such living possible.

Preaching Pathways

1. **Grace is more powerful than you think.** Grace is the *gift* of new life—new resurrection life. But grace is also the *invitation* to live in a new way, a way that leads to life. And finally, grace is more than the invitation; it is the *power* to live in this new way, to put it into practice in our relationships with others.

2. **New life takes practice.** One of the great mysteries of the gospel is how salvation belongs to the Lord—it is *his* work—and yet he invites us into it. This is why the New Testament implores us to exert effort, to join God's work by learning new habits, new patterns of behavior. Yet even our work, even our participation is a grace; it is possible only by the power of the Holy Spirit.

3. **Self-giving love results in relationships of mutuality.** One of the best ways to check how well this new life is taking root in us is to take an inventory of our relationships. How do we treat those less powerful than we are? How do we treat those who are more powerful than we are? Even if the structures are not *equal*, the love and respect—the compassion, kindness, humility, gentleness, and patience—can be *mutual*.

4:2-6

Relationship With The World Around Us

(Amber Ayers)

Two imperatives are employed in Paul's final instructions to the Colossians: "Devote yourselves to prayer" (v. 2) and "Be wise in the way you act toward outsiders" (v. 5). Both pertain to Christ-followers as missionaries in an "everyday" context.

"Effective evangelism begins with persevering prayer,"[1] fueled by gratitude. A prayerless church is at risk of the enemy creeping in with destruction and division that undermines the spread of the gospel message. It is likely that the Colossians had grown sleepy; and like the disciples in the Garden of Gethsemane who failed to "watch and pray" (Matt. 26:41), we too are admonished to continue steadfastly in prayer with thanksgiving.

As a minority in a hostile environment, much like our context today, Paul was concerned with the impressions the Colossians made on their neighbors, especially when the door of opportunity opened for them to share their faith in Christ. The Greek word *kairos* means "the opportune

---

1   R.C. Lucas, *Fullness and Freedom: The Message of Colossians and Philemon* (Downers Grove: InterVarsity Press, 1980), 171.

time, the right moment." And the verb *exagorazō* means "to buy out" or "to buy up" (v. 5). Like zealous bargain hunters, Christians are to "buy up the opportune time" lest the opportunity to share the gospel slips out of our hands.

Three characteristics should govern the speech of those who follow Christ: 1) Their words should always be gracious. 2) Their speech is to be salty. 3) They should be ready with answers to those who question and challenge their faith (v. 6). Let's look at these characteristics one at a time.

First, "gracious speech" means that our words are civil and compassionate, the product of active and sensitive listening. The Greek word for grace, *charis*, like in English, carries the double meaning of both God's grace and human graciousness.[2] The walls that unbelievers put up can only be broken down through God's grace and by exemplification in human graciousness. In stark contrast to the sins of speech in verses 8-9, gracious speech builds up and brings life.

Second, "salty speech" idiomatically refers to the three basic uses of salt in biblical times: preservation, purification and flavor. Conversation that preserves the joy, dignity and wonder of life should be a regular part of the believer's interactions. Words that stain and smear are unworthy of the disciple of Jesus, but words that cleanse and purify were to be on the lips of the Colossians and are just as desperately needed today. And what comes out of the mouth of a believer should be witty

---

2   Wright, 153.

and lively, bringing flavor to those around them. The Christianity that stodgily depresses or unimaginatively bores people is too common. The Colossians are commanded to bear the name of Christ with piquancy and zest.

Third, because the Colossians were in a contentious context, Paul encourages them to have their answers ready for those outside the faith. This final phrase builds upon the preceding exhortations. The person who makes the most of every opportunity (v. 5) will offer gracious and salty responses (v. 6) to any sincere query or malicious challenge facing the church.[3]

Preaching Pathways

1. **When the door of opportunity opens, walk through it!** How often do we make the excuse, "Oh, I can't take the time, maybe when I'm not so busy"? We find that the door of opportunity slams shut as quickly as it opened. It is a tragedy when a door is opened but the Word of Christ is not proclaimed. Doors are opening and closing all around us, and we must pray for the sensitivity to see and the courage to speak. Someone new moves into the neighborhood—an open door for friendship. A friend is faced with unemployment or a scary medical diagnosis—an open door for support and assurance.

3   Robert W. Wall, *IVP New Testament Commentary Series: Colossians and Philemon* (Downers Grove: InterVarsity Press, 1993), 168.

A conversation turns from surface-level issues to a deep lack of meaning in life—an open door for sharing faith.[4]

2. **The marginalization of the church is not to be resented but embraced as evangelistic opportunity.** The mission field is no longer thousands of miles away; it's at our doorstep. Picture these words over the exit sign of the church or on the way out of the parking lot: "You are now entering your mission field." Because the church no longer sits at the center of society, we must posture ourselves as missionaries in a foreign land, like the Colossians. This doesn't require theological gymnastics; it means we simply let our words and actions communicate the love of Jesus to those around us.

3. **Speak life.** Listen to the Lord, actively listen to those around you, and then speak wise and healing words, stewarding your syllables and using everything spoken for good.[5]

---

4   Demarest, 182.

5   Brady Boyd, *Speak Life* (Colorado Springs: David C. Cook, 2016), 15.

4:7-18

The Gift of Kingdom Friendship

(Daniel Grothe)

A good book knows how to come in for a good landing, and the letter to the Colossian believers lands just right.

In the minds of many today, the Apostle Paul looms large as a mythical figure. We read about his great miracles, we ponder the gospel mysteries he so powerfully articulated, and we are awestruck by his dramatic conversion. *This is God's man!* After two millennia and a few thousand miles of geographical and cultural separations, it would be easy for us to simply mythologize him. So doing, we run the risk of losing his humanity.

But the close of Colossians won't let us get away with any romanticizing or mythologizing of Paul's life. Instead, we find Paul's frail humanity leaking out of the pen and all over the page. He's writing from prison, a place of great introspection and reflection, and what comes out of him? His memory of his friends.

He talks about Tychicus, "a beloved brother...faithful minister...fellow servant" (v. 7). Paul was sending Tychicus to deliver the Colossian letter and to encourage the believers there (v. 8). Onesimus, the former slave who ran away from Philemon, was a recent convert of Paul's and was being sent back to Colossae with Tychicus. Along with our present letter, Tychicus and Onesimus were also carrying the letter to Philemon. Paul ached that both his friends, as well as the letters they were carrying, would be warmly received, which is evidenced by how personal he gets here. He mentions Aristarchus and Mark and Jesus/Justus, "the only Jewish believers among my co-workers" (v. 11a). He mentions Epaphras and Luke and Demas. He mentions his friends in the Laodicean church. He remembers Nympha and the church meeting in her house. He remembers Archippus. And what's the last thing Paul begs them to do? *"Remember* my chains." He is saying: "Don't forget me. *Please*, don't forget me."

Paul "fought with wild beasts at Ephesus" (1 Cor. 15:32), a moment of persecution that was a life-threatening exchange. He describes himself "hard pressed on every side, but not crushed; perplexed, but not in despair; persecuted, but not abandoned; struck down, but not destroyed" (2 Cor. 4:8-9). During one stretch of his ministry, the apostle would be shipwrecked and snake-bitten, imprisoned and falsely accused (Acts 27-28). Clearly, Paul was no stranger to times of deep loneliness and isolation. Small wonder that at that moment, in the bottom of a prison cell, Paul remembers his friends. *"And what a comfort they have been!"* (v. 11b, emphasis added).

For all of Colossians' vivid imagery and world-shaping theology, we should not think of it as a purely *theological* document, as a mere *conceptual* defense of Jesus the Cosmic Christ. As they say, "The proof of the pudding is in the tasting," and our closing section gives us a taste test of what the Lordship of Christ actually *does* in someone's life. It leads them to friendship! Paul is no Lone Ranger apostle gallivanting around the countryside in apostolic isolation. He's a man rooted in relationship, a man who doesn't seem to go anywhere alone. He's got friends and colleagues and dear companions, people whom he's encouraging and people who are encouraging him.

The work of God does not go forward at the hands of the marketing strategists who know how to "get the word out" about God. The work of God is not done simply by theological program. What Colossians 4:7-18 helps us understand is that the work of God is carried out in the world through *friendship*, through groups of people who have believed what has been taught, who have steeped their lives in the reality of Jesus, and who have linked arms with each other to carry that message into the uttermost bounds of the earth.

Preaching Pathways

1. **Hope for our lonely world.** In a world of hyper-connection and shallow relationships, Colossians 4:7-18 holds great promise. Life can be lonely—*ministry* can be lonely—and people are longing for the kind of comforting relationships that Paul mentions in verse 11b. As preachers, we can work with that longing and show people how to live into the richness of relationship.

2. **Kingdom relationship.** Kingdom relationships aren't just about

hanging out with other people who share our beliefs. These relationships ought to lead to rich discipleship. In the list of names found in Colossians 4:7-18, we find people whom Paul converted and people who were rough around the edges. Paul himself was in need of people to make him a more faithful follower of Jesus. The back-and-forth of friendships ought to lead to a maturing of our faith. This is a great opportunity to remind the congregation about the spiritual disciplines involved in spiritual growth—prayer, Scripture, and service.

Bibliography

Barclay, William. *The New Daily Study Bible: The Letters to the Philippians, Colossians and Thessalonians*. Louisville: Westminster John Knox Press, 2003. (Part of the New Daily Study Bible series, this commentary skillfully brings the results of scholarship to the ordinary reader. Although originally written in a male-dominated culture, the editors improved the series with gender-neutral language.)

Boyd, Brady. *Speak Life.* Colorado Springs: David C. Cook, 2016. (Boyd speaks a practical and winsome word to a culture mired in toxic, divisive ways of speaking. Very helpful for thinking about how our words can be used to build up and not tear down.)

Demarest, Gary. *Colossians: The Mystery of Christ in Us.* Waco: Word, Incorporated, 1979. (This commentary emerges out of 25+ years of pastoral experience. Demarest shows the reader how the wisdom of the Apostle Paul for the Colossians is just as applicable today as it was in ancient biblical times.)

Garland, David E. *The NIV Application Commentary: Colossians and Philemon*. Grand Rapids: Zondervan, 1998. (Part of the NIV Application Commentary Series, this volume helps the reader bring the ancient message of Colossians into a modern context. Each passage is viewed through three lenses: original meaning, bridging contexts, and contemporary significance.)

Lincoln, Andrew. *The New Interpreter's Bible: Volume 11 (Colossians).* Nashville: Abingdon Press, 2000. (A commentary engaging the primary movements within the letter. Professor Lincoln also helpfully provides readable introductory essays on relevant background information for the letter.)

Lucas, R.C. *Fullness and Freedom: The Message of Colossians and Philemon.* Downers Grove: InterVarsity Press, 1980. (This exposition illuminates the work of the Spirit that is necessary for the life, growth and health of churches.)

Moo, Douglas J. *The Letters to the Colossians and to Philemon: Pillar New Testament Commentary.* Grand Rapids: Wm. B. Eerdmans Publishing Co., 2008. (A thorough exegetical commentary that will delight and help student, pastor, and scholar alike.)

Newbigin, Lesslie. *The Gospel in a Pluralist Society.* Grand Rapids: Wm. B. Eerdmans Publishing Co., 1989. (One would be hard-pressed to find a finer articulation and defense of the role of the local fellowship of believers as the visible embodiment of the gospel than this classic by the great Anglican bishop and missiologist, Lesslie Newbigin.)

Ogilvie, Lloyd John. *You Are Loved and Forgiven.* Ventura: Regal Books, 1977. (A gifted preacher and warm-hearted pastor, Ogilvie sheds light on the ancient text to the church in Colossae. He prepared for the writing of this book by submerging himself in Colossians, venturing his own translation of the original Greek text, preaching it to his own congregation, and then finally prepared a contemporary message for our time.)

Pao, David W. *Colossians and Philemon: Exegetical Commentary on the New Testament.* Grand Rapids: Zondervan, 2012. (This series is written both for the scholar and the lay student of Scripture. Accessible and helpful.)

Wall, Robert W. *IVP New Testament Commentary Series: Colossians and Philemon.* Downers Grove: InterVarsity Press, 1993. (Part of the IVP New Testament Commentary Series, this work beautifully joins the scholarly perspective with a pastoral heart.)

Wright, N. T. *Colossians and Philemon: Tyndale New Testament Commentary Series.* Downers Grove: InterVarsity Press, 1986. (Wright brings his classic erudition, clear writing, and pastoral sensitivity to bear in this commentary. Highly recommended.)

Wright, N. T. *Paul for Everyone: Ephesians, Philippians, Colossians and Philemon.* Louisville: Westminster John Knox Press, 2015. (Wright doing what Wright does best: combining pastoral insights with his scholarly expertise on the life of Jesus and the world of the New Testament. He is a compulsory conversation partner whose prayerful thoughts will fuel your own.)

Made in the USA
Middletown, DE
06 February 2019